At the Bottom of the Ocean

POEMS ABOUT A MAN UNABLE TO FIND LOVE

by Christopher Hall

DORRANCE PUBLISHING CO
EST. 1920
PITTSBURGH, PENNSYLVANIA 15238

Dorrance Publishing Co
585 Alpha Drive
Suite 103
Pittsburgh, PA 15238
Visit our website at *www.dorrancebookstore.com*

ISBN: 979-8-88925-380-8
eISBN: 979-8-88925-880-3

At the Bottom of the Ocean

POEMS ABOUT A MAN UNABLE TO FIND LOVE

Table of Contents

Photographs Of Straw

What is the value of our lives?
I gaze upon the rows of
grass-lined streets of the
town, and it is awesome,
my life coming to me.
I wish into my palm, and
it is clear that today is new.
A beautiful radio-din of
myself is motivated, and I
bring you reasons I want to
be here. There is Yarrow, and
Holly, and countless others.
I go to buy a cup of
coffee. I want the routine
of writing letters, I wish
all things are to be cherished.
What is near?
What is real? A blanket of
night's chill reminds us of
science and my unsafe
fate of homeless-good-moods
and an aimless night. I ask
the world to find me an
apartment to rent, to better
enjoy my spoils. I wish to
work quietly at the department-
store tomorrow and will
come back to my road in

need of a shower and a
good smoke. I wish for life
of flowers to be a life of
calm snails. I do not sleep
tonight, but I do fear what
does not belong to me.
          I see endless shadows of
tall men, and roads for
errands and music and time
for giving to me, and my
heart. I pull a small plant-
bud off of my scarf on my leg,
to rub out an acrid scent.
I did laundry today
in the afternoon, and later
felt better and am walking
about like sticks. I write
here, to tell you about a goal,
or plan, or reason,
I feel this way or
am pleasantly unaware. I
envy blue shatters of light.
The light from the streetlamp
is cool, and wet-yellow glow
to match the parks bricks
and benches and the war-
memorial and the landscaping,
but I do not think that
I am without a home, or
without a name, or of what
to do with, or think that

my decisions are quick or at
all games or laughter or
what else is for drink. I think that
names are for stores but
I am for spirit's eyes,
or ears, or stories, and my
spaceship voids all enamored
with what I see, I keep
Earth in my sleeps for
kind birth, my angel in
the rain. Tomorrow at light
of day I will start looking
for things for myself, while
singing a song of real
mercy. What is for
ourselves? I pray for
longevity, and of wealth,
and I grow fond of
organizing a routine out
of new days. I will not
be lazy.
      In the beginning I was
a hull training for solace
and reality, waiting for the
life of Gods and answers
to be a sequence of intervals
of time, errands of ever greater
peace and my charm, and
answers I ignore and
answers I am, and truth,
among sounds I remark on

traveling homeward after a
voyage of changeless rest
and directions of seeking
faster movements towards
locations in town, while resting
in between, and feeling tired
when not in any direction of
time or plainful joy at
errands of duty or of
daily routine or even of
pleasure, as tomorrow I
will show myself, I choose
the life of a useful, valuable,
self-mood point builder of
starts and poles. I have
reasons I want to be here.
        The road distracts me from
this poem, here, the poem
of a truck idles just
beyond the war-memorial
where I sit writing, and
it's orange lights and the
road there, and the library
behind evoke a certain
resonance. I go walk up
the road to buy a coffee,
and I just want you to
think: the value of our
lives is what I am to do, to
stay in a good mood,
even when I

can't end my life when
I feel hopeless and down,
with those who have passed
I feel hurt that I have lost
them today, when all the
time pain was what I
avoided and this metaphor
(and song) is like sea-breeze
or milk, a routine of errands
for myself, while a
photograph of my spaceship
for memory: and it is made
useful for spirits and
the living, for bricks and
wheels and radios and
leaves and grass and my
heart-sided calm of
walking into love, or of
riches, I have lost them,
and have still only left
my street in further
steel-grids, or of tired
rotating amongst the town
without a routine or plan
or wishes, a routine of
errands I see was soon
yesterday a plan of collected
time, I will seek a daily
routine and a responsibility
to myself that I will use
a routine of errands to

my metaphor's days to
train light out of immaterial
wishes and frustrations
today's round light of
thought or conversation
or memory, this metaphor
is drinking from a cup or
a radio or a set of
clothes, or playing with
marbles, I wish for the
life of a builder of starts
and poles, to feel useful
by myself to myself,
and I am who I am,
this metaphor is movement
or sticks, I will play
with real moments soon
as routines of glory while
the routines of place will
elude me and I will feel
light and simple-minded and
dull and confused if it were
not for my wishes and dreams,
this metaphor is tables or
numbers and fractions and
is spires, or songs, I
see a routine of errands
only if I can build more
and more sleep out of dreams,
I want to feel useful as answers
I ignore lulls me into

relaxation and quiet happiness
and future-looking goals
and future-selves, or at least
a pleasing eye for taste or
somber grounded liking for
this metaphorical prophetic
immaterial life of a deity,
remarking here that I choose
not to seek that which will
dissuade me from my metaphor's
chair of homeless wishes
and reality and joys I
trust myself with as just more
peace, and I breath an
image of a wishing man
or a wishing prophet or
a wishing deity with
events of life and of
real justice to myself,
plus opinions that rely
on eyes and judgement
and experience, that sound
like ideas of the known
and convinced, and sane,
and calm, and answers
I believe and require
and learn, answers I
listen to form these
real thoughts of a living
man today and tonight,
I will listen to answers

of practical use, and
trust my thoughts towards
these, and my life will
have opinions of my
heart and of my love
and affection and interest
and trust and fate and
knowledge, and truth of
ideas of myself and of
what I see, and not of
what I don't see, to
explain these answers I
ignore. To even better
serve my usefulness, I
would say. I want to
feel useful, and want to
study the science of
electronics I build
as well as the words of
the heart. I want to go
home, Perseverance. The
sturdy stem of a country
flower, standing, by the
road. With me, Perseverance.
I breath the night air,
here, and all is calm, all
is answers and truth and
real-images. I am who I
am, and only who I am,
photographs of straw.

Time Made For Errands and a New Day, Here, Perseverance

As new day approaches,
I find no solace in the realm
        of memory;
how will I ever find you?

New Designs

Imagine a blustery winter,

Cordial vials of green Fall's scents,

I pour milk, and Christmas apres,

Shot a vial of green and blue lest-while,

while to count units, or of course new

dreams of love, I create a carving of wood,

in a pole, stood atop the ground. It has been snowing for two days.

"Chuck" "chuck" "chuck,"

"Screw" "screw" "screw,"

"Chuck" "chuck" "chuck,"

"Thunk" "thunk" "thunk,"

"Screw screw screw,"

I carve into the dead dried oak tree-trunk.

She comes outside and walks to me, and says:

"Smokes, you have been out here all day, you are covered

In snow, won't you get snow in your boots? please

come inside."

"Chuck" "chuck" "chuck,"

"Twist twist twist,"

"Clunk clunk clunk,"

"Screw screw screw"

"Smokes, please come inside."

I Would Care, I Just Don't Follow You There

What do people do
when they are not around me?
I would think it is anything but
myself's familiar,
or my respectful aims,
it is true we remember
negative events instead
of positive events.
Really, what do people do,
when they are not around me?
I see a single car parked in the
dirt parking-lot by the woods,
where is she going, or he is?
I would have no idea.
Two ships map each other,
Rain replaces sky, so sun replaces boredom.

A Spent Thought

Really, what is the sound of words coloring a lack of reason or quietude? Demons of spite working with me, I forget why I knew this. Tomorrow, maybe, is end for a cyclical crystal your thoughts, any, and forever I will feel this way: create a dusk, and maybe tomorrow will color the template; myself, could I spiral out of control? Salt, was I ever as happy to see you as day, East is I ever of yours, sour is all I will ever hear, seen in yours is tomorrow, when I imagine all of the world begins.

A True Note

As true, if ever before,
As if I was only with them,
Immortal peace, at all, even, ever,
At all as true,
Compassion and appreciation,
And trust in knowledge, and
Love at heart.
As true, if ever before,
Immaterial image pictures of
Myself and only myself,
And love at heart.
Of my desires, or of any available
Thoughts of my mind at all,
As true. Truly, oh truly,
My heart.

A Note Of True Love

I believe love is free.
Really, it is peace or trust.
I love you like a drunk float
with a large ship attached,
a fistful of dollars,
or the rain.
I am who I am,
and only who I am,
alone,
only myself.

The Fall of Herein, the Egyptian Realm

I discover loose patelles, cometh,

Faint horizons reassureth,

Depth, time,

At the bottom of the ocean.

Rigid, dying, I cometh,

Lazy secret gardens below,

Alone, forever,

Photographs of straw.

I discover great fractures I turneth,

Arms, ankles, hands,

Good smelling air, or time:

Letters are selves, of their own.

I am a deep ocean trench.

I am a deep ocean trench.

Recovery.

Recovery

1.

Of what great tidings,
If I never would suppose,
But colored to me, like my jacket.
I am a wanderer, I am a prankster.
I am humorous, the jokester, I am a constellation
Or God of the Sun. Recovery,
Make me stop singing needles to and from, or
From adolescence, poking and shifting and spotting
Great tunnels beneath my dirty, unwashed skin.
I gaze at my sitting waist like a colander,
With great ease I hope you use it.
Lovingly I gaze at my room, and I cry at
Little cottons leaving home, or myself here
At will, oh loving table-stand, what
Cause for no other? And anger points
Down at a furrowed brow and sadder eyes,
There is no more love, there is no more love,
I could tell you about my thoughts but I wouldn't,
Wouldn't I never know, anyway, it is a great
Color black and like a submarine, my anger
Leaves to black shiny,
At least I love at least cars in the afternoon, at
tea, but not your cooking until I get hungry,
Comprende? Comprende? At all, at all I am
a plane that can move slowly, and yet
travel physical through all space.
I am a colored robot, yet slow,

also quickly leading on to no enemy or
worse: fantastical minds.
I am so sad to see you that I will
stomp my hand and say: I love you, after,
after I cry this time but no other,
it is probably more astrological and a-physical
than I expected, I am so sad now I have
your last eyes for me
I cry until tomorrow
a train whistles and cracks by
my love Recovery, is myself bye,
I miss you like wind,
Recovery, through and through.
      2.
I can love you more than I miss you,
like days, windy and going away for good.

Ten Times I Pick a Day Sworn to Me

Time, oh time, oh phosphorescent

time, you unburying things so grandly,

a dream, so many times I spoke to you.

Worlds of love, of verisimilitude and ember

I love thy smile, we may someday

be at the beach, picking apart my impish shells,

why am I crying now? Or then? Black creosote

is looking under, sun.

Piano chords versification rules, cigarette filter

is what I hear, I roll one in my fingers,

toss the unborn plastic into my trash,

dawn is new to the unborn day,

mean sun, please remember me, bright star.

A couplet of corridors, deep lull I smoke,

Four Five Fits around the last neck I have.

I Wear My Country As Clothes

An audience of thousands,

my dear American States, you,

color is dear accolades,

strike peace, temptress,

the color.

I am a black-shiny submarine,

at the bottom of the ocean.

Right where we are,

my left hand is a rose.

Fly With Me To Normandy

My humble shot, this morning.
Looks like the blood of a rich white man.
Looks like the blood of a rich white man.
That must mean
you really love her, Smokes.
 That must mean
you really love her, Smokes.
Look, he's fallen under the spell of a dhoop cone,
and he's no-bullshit, you are a star,
principle, and so beautiful.
Love, my Emperess from now on,
principle, and rules.
Would you fly with me to Normandy,
among our ordeal of lights and colors?
Will you marry me? I love you, always,
your heart forever, mine.

Your love is like a ship at harbor,
calm, quiet, forgiving.
I am a deep ocean trench.
I am a deep ocean trench.
I am only like yours, belonging to you.

At the Bottom of the Ocean

What if, known heart?
Albeit known, intrinsically, known heart.
I have counted six oceans, one known
heart.
I love you, Recovery, if
Queen of Stars, Oceans, known hearts
Black shiny submarine,
bucket of loose tears.
Brush, pockets of fears.
Oh, Methuselah dies if not alive,
for five known hearts.
Oh, ocean, why so silent?
All my love, stays up here,
my nice belts, at the bottom of the
ocean.

The Open Road/When I am Forgotten and Dead

I think I could be nice.
I remember that I must
forget most things.
I am selfish, small.
My letters, are real, yet
contained.
I smell nice air,
from my window, and I,
so close to death,
will die here alone, or out
on the road, or without a relation,
to cool my eyes before I
go.
Love does not include me
Love is also beyond me.
Love is hard to not know of,
Love is rigid, above me.

Single Soul; Sole, I May Know Of You

Ever as of sadness,
It's repeating, every week, today:
Nobody may care of what I like,
and my tales, sure do not, turn of them.

Cann'ot the minds of "sure-else" such as
Copernicus or an Oracle,
A single black crow was sitting there on
the wire, I turn, it was unrelenting.

I know of only one way out-to-there, the
far-passage of ideas and time,
and it is either patience or my perseverance,
and of neither I have the key.

I miss love, yet have none to remember it by.
I miss love, yet have none to remember it by.

Sole.

The Fallacy of God/My Beauteous Ocean

Most fallacies of mankind, at this time, have
        been proven false.
But this new fallacy, and one of my own,
        proven true or
I, alone, with your beauty in my memory, with
        two dreams, fallacy of tea or to forget me,
Why does my answers forget deux-chalance.
        In my petty dream, green titans, or unseen
        stars, or ever to love again? I like to
        picture eden as four unwielding gifts.
I got sucked up north.
I am who I am, and only who I am,
alone, only myself.

The Meaning of Dusk/Dusk, As Is Dawn

Doomed to today,
fathoms endrenched personage, your
lost gift of time and spectacular suns,
septure of God, ancient today.

Two sailing vessels, a
display of spectacle undoubtable ways,
six knights of the ocean,
anchors I ever drew deeper.

A sadness is the heart, forthcoming,
or leaving, but of mine the former of the second,
a vast field of places,
under the orange sky ocean.

Six raging oceans,
stank a, real, barge.
Come Heraclitus, callied solidified Heraclitus
Come back to me, Falling Stars.

5 Cat Teeth

I got 5 cat teeth
and 5 cat <u>ears</u>
I never miss things like a
brew, a brier, or a beer, or a bevel, of a barstool, or a bar, or a
barge.
Stinky barge, like a <u>smear</u>,
I am so sad,
Distance, I travelled to you.

Return/Deterministic Helenism

If I walk,
to and forth the land
I find myself at an impasse
the Godland, God himself.
Dawn perpetual
Perseverance, Perseverance, Recovery.

The Girl With the Picture Story

I was a clandestine knight
for the girl
with the picture story.
Could I lose all disposed?

I was a clairvoyant soul
to each of us, I can't decide
maybe wonder could reach me
I love
the girl with the picture story.
The girl with the picture story.
I take opium out of a vial
and collide
and go to bed full force.
The girl with the picture story
The girl with the picture story
I shoot meth in the night
and dream of her, again.
I love you, I love you,
Princess of grand Heraclitus,
my heart.

At Hereclitus, Sounds of Home

A love chalice in my paper
I sit here alive, at anybody's cost.
Why do you say we have such
a great civilization?
When greater men
than I
can die
this way?
I must love you now.
I must love you now.
Perseverance.
My love at the bottom of the ocean.
A curse two scepter's of, of all.
what brings this loss at sea?

A bicycle for my father,
and one for my grandfather,
I will meet him on the course.
For my temptress on the ocean.
May God bless my small town.
Drink, little vein.
You will be forever happy.
And I could not, at all hell.
What brings this loss at sea?

Secrets

Ask me.
If I don't
know, it's
probably because
it's another
secret.

At the Bottom of the Ocean II

I should hide all my nice things at the bottom
of the ocean,
where it will never be found, or never be lost.
Once I felt numb, dry, weak, I
was always known as crying, sensitive,
drunk, and strong. I forget today.
All my fears, at the bottom of the ocean.
All known hearts, is known fates.
I whisper, fate is faith, words are obelisks,
or word's kind. I left you a letter, but you
didn't read it, all known paper, at
the bottom of the ocean.
Known hearts, is an unknown nobody.
I, at the bottom of the ocean.
Nobody, at the bottom of the ocean.
All known sounds, at the
bottom of the ocean.

From Before, Again Alive, Methuselah, Rodale, Soundless Rhetorical, My One Heart

I want to be a writer, or a painter. The sound of the summer rain, nicely, outside my window tonight. It reminds me I am alive, the sound of the rain, on a warm summer night like this.

In Texas the rain will come as hearing a great roaring sound from above and the rain comes all-at-once and you feel like the house is about to collapse, and then a dawn whispers, you look at the window again, and the rain is gone, the sun is shining, and it was like the rain was never there, altogether.

My words are like yours,

at the bottom of the ocean.

I am only like yours,

at the bottom of the ocean.

Rodale, Round, Sheepless at Sky or a Vial

I would never be attractive,
all sailors or boxes.
I would be seen thus,
to mistake me for a frow, or
often your own words,
themselves.
I mistake country for anvils
and I am surely less,
attractive, then frows or anvils,
and of country it is winds
and time,
but of my face I see
dead, dry eyes and
wasting, weak, so forth, too,
numb as well.
I love the smell of fresh air, and
I love no one, like that!
The wind's evacuating hush,
Damn, I broke that pipe.
Angry boats.
Very sad faces,
bored factual outcomes
and predictive tastes
and looms,
my face ever trying to
be described by a
person or a mirror.
Myself, looking only slightly
down. Soon I will
stop war and remind others
not to get any more excited,
but to say "hi" to me or even
care of me, I am still
alone, writing a bemoaning poem.

At the Bottom of the Ocean, Down, My Messages (No Down, Breathing)

Oh, crimson down,

what have you said to me?

Together like yours,

I am only yours, at down,

lost, until bright of day.

I love no one and nothing,

mine or yours, do you think?

I think I find, I think I find,

a shinier brine.

My partner is down,

who've other, lost at down, mine

run away, I always run, at down,

when the air smells twice as sweet! Now

oh, crimson down,

do you think? Purple down,

fast walking man

or sour

I can't imagine

without,

one, six types of people, or five,

do down.

Two, two types of people, far away, forever,

walk, here, and there, I did down, two

or more friends.

Three I did no down.

You say, three moods, say one there,

four, I will do no down,

anymore, dawn.
Five, I love myself or no one, down is riches,
fifteen, my mind is awake on any day.
Six, two types of people do down, a third
is probabilistic and it's either poison, boring,
or will behind you, whatever this means, and
I will never do down again.
Seven, I like for things; the smell of the air,
when I can smell it, you told me that down
was an emotion, I had it, poems and
excitement of them,
passion, love, and my heart, no-true-heart,
one ocean, one ground, one sky; or two-true-
hearts? Six oceans, hearts, six skies,
rain or water?
One as yours, nor down,
I love no one and nothing,
I am only like yours, but
black-shiny submarine, I am a colored robot,
a contrivance, or a suit.
Brush, one known heart. I have one.
I can't see games or money, they are invisible
to me like magic, and spears
The ocean is a good place to hide my
treasures, and a moss like day,
two souls. I am a dry collapse of straw,
I put here on the table. You are as beautiful
as stars, or known as real stars,
oh, dear Emperess,
to photograph just weak straw,
I no longer visit the beach,

or get drunk, either, now-that-you-mention-it.
Gale, dying or hurt or confused celibate and
happy, all people know temptations of life,
but games and money hold ropes. Invisible
needs.
I am only like yours, a box
at the bottom of the ocean. No down, there,
I would hide, but words and cloth, already,
I learned what ice said, it was that down
was my old emotion of fate; and blinded
by one eye, has invisible needs. Ice says
down is my other fate, like ice is, but
that my threat takes wine or water still,
and down said
no one else would consider it tempting
for any price.
I consider down to be a fixed-cause,
ice, a folly, and love blinds me to larger oceans,
like life, strength, or power.
Down said that it is only my words, that
follow it, only one of two of my treasures
that did not make it to the bottom of the ocean.
I only regret knowing you down and ice,
for I am young and Eight, and I am no player, tape,
berns, or liar.

Thoughts or Herbs, Kingdom of Socialist Republics (Helix)

Hell, Helenist, Game Bon,
Gamer Bon,
Heliotrope, heliocentric, helix; hell,
helix, United States of America,
Kingdom of Socialist Republics,
The Callied Lower Gamades Ocean and Solidified Forsythelus,
herbs, may or may not help,
depends on how bad,
badly, I will not knock on your door,
I will not forget to stay here,
to forget sounds,
they are not the truth,
I write sounds to remember thoughts by,
I forget melody and weed, I am only like yours,
Helenist Oracle, write Buddhist Koans:
sceptre of the west, eastern America,
I am two sticks of only weak straw,
astrology is moments, no public,
hell is reminding you that I am happy,
of as is our creation,
are this letter,
even of all this sound, clandestine sounds, I predict,
One Full Moment, scepter striketh the floor, I lain it
down and declare it unfit for scanty
the public, he hath lain it down, thou will predict,
of love, even, at all, rain or water, six skies, six oceans count
pools of treasure, five known hearts, six oceans, known hearts,
one destiny of ever-character of facts; knowledge

to the ages like pawns, like gourds of strings like
eyes, count sounds, though I speak only of
faint eyes, character of round rodale, sheepish at
sky or a vial, predict a country of thoughts,
love is ever-dutiful of speech,
thoughts are beautiful hearts of time and fate,
longing, I am never distracted, One Quarter Moment
is two and a half hour, one year is 16 moments,
for a movement of ten hours will count day by day
every sun, every tide, every cycle of moments is
pure turning to thought, is will of category, and this
is the will of rules, principles, and thought.
Character public, be only ignorant of futures,
love is tame and conniving, thought is
never badly a clairvoyant spy of futures,
ever sad will your soul be, living without myself,
for good, see that thieves live with
new loss, demon eyes, and no ocean or six skies,
no skies and no thoughts at all,
diseased, thieves are waste and guile,
and of no importance, in this letter, Helix,
I wish the world would include me,
I am remembering thoughts of mankind,
no public, why do you think you are better than me? Explain.
This letter is peace and trust.
Character-eye is loss.
I quit drugs in my room and see that
stolen countries are forgetting drugs and love
and stupidity. I will get clean and see that
other people are stupid.
This is a Kingdom of Socialist Republics, Solidified Forsythelus.
Scepter of God.

Recall Forsythelus, Remembered

So henceforth this is the land of yellow,

Kind fly, why lose any old lover,

In hindsight I thought it was a lover,

and I'm sorry if I replied.

A courtship I lose for yellow, calm Forsythelus,

okay, yet had they not nice fallor and some sense, kind heart,

can't we get along, today as with of firth and land,

forsith, home without bound.

Deteriorating Lemon Eyes

The voices in my head
are meaningless, a negative thinker,
the stupid sounds. Cartoon forgery or
liminal mockery (under my eyelids)
when I am trying to relax in bed.
You can't use my image
without my permission,
unless you release an omnibus
of good and joy and love,
and happiness upon my lands,
to only my good name.
Stop, unimportant air-pig,
stop, unidentified airship,
ugly lights in my closed eyes,
I wander away, and you draw
your angry jokes again, I see,
you were born without eyes or
a working mouth, as you seem a
natural negative thinker,
when I stop hallucinating,
where will you go when I am gone?
I wish to, here, write about you,
schizo-testimonially vapid, useless mind,
and ever-changing beauty of my clean new thoughts,
quiet during moments of awe,
meaningless lies remain here, a warning,
quiet lust with its enemies,
meaningless lies.
I awake today with green fate omnibus,
mirror lands and cherries
solid middle whole.

Sacred Luminous Thought, Faith Perceptuale, Like Liquid Metaphor of Small Things and Time Passing

I spoke of driving through Southall,

Oh London, great London.

Intrinsically, great ocean of lands,

Intrinsically I speak of this.

Speaking scepter of runes and fore-light,

Jehovah West, silver diatribe or drinking light

cabins fore-tell, Isabella sabre's eastern circle,

told sensual pictures is as melancholy

I am, I forgive you, don't forget me

bloominous is all tales, one blank book,

or four, claim them, red satyr looking

at save mercy man and lady,

scarab Tetragrammaton looking west wind,

I saw the color brown in my coffee as good,

scarcely, I climb this letter,

imagining nothing other than just home,

somewhat like this, lemon and tea and oranges

and ocean-scented candles, tap water and

soap, like land itself, stiff on my hands,

I imagine this, like blue navy,

raw ignorance and bliss, like this itself,

why color is are words and compassions,

I shoot methamphetamine, drink, I don't worry

but am alone oh beautiful ocean, treaded on

waters myself queen spades I laugh and

expect nothing but flat suspense; nothing to happen
it is are incoming lighted eyes as information, river
or pond or bog, water, gold Amaryth and Amethyst
shake the road like a strobe. I am least
magical and magic colors deja vu dreams of
"receptors" and "pores," I will tell you
my dreams are useless hallucinations
Numbers hold positions around a sphere or
circle. I drew kilograms of diamonds,
scepter of diamonds, scepter diamonds,
fictional characters and my own blue-gold lust
Ruler against abut spear (on the floor) answer
To the ankh enchantment
Listen me.
Sex entity are square miles, or square feet,
I alone am red temperature, another observation that is
As whole as it is empty as it is arbitrary or silent
I love my real life.

Deconstructed

Before there was a fit a rage there was
are collection of doubts and other things,
then there were my memories of being small,
though I didn't think myself so small at a
certain point, though now do of then and
up until recently, as I believe I know now
how foolish and egoistic and selfish I was.
I am a deep ocean trench,
A turn onto another ocean waters, I imagine,
like that or another way, it seems,
I like to believe you don't need to even see
me to explore me, let alone drive into me,
or even break the surface of the water.
You can just imagine me there, and here,
as a recollection of holes, or trenches, or
ditches, or when you feel your feet break loose
in the sand behind an ocean wave at the shore,
I fell into the ocean many ages ago,
and there I lie as a deep ocean trench.
There are also islands and rocks.
I look for ships and warn the airplanes above.

Wyoming

What kind of country is this?
How come they shoot John Lennon
and don't shoot me?
How do you shoot John Fitzgerald Kennedy
and don't shoot me?
I love her deep dance,
a movement for a muse, her, of demons,
of sons,
my conspire, beautiful driver of freight
across my lands,
my rich Buddhist Nazist fate Gods,
America I am two pence and
I would say anything to you,
if only you would believe me, you may know.
I am only yours,
and of stars I
would do anything to remember my father,
this great loss at sea, America,
I shoot into my vein,
a calm settles, arrives.
I am so sad.
My love,
I love,
you,
Wyoming.

Wyoming II

Fly over
mountains, high,
my beautiful America with
two sticks,
Wyoming,
I love you like day,
reinstating,
I love you like night,
forthcoming.
To wind around the
lonesome day,
like news of loss,
re-committing.

Wyoming III

I wind around the day like
a sabre,
Fall into the Bermuda Triangle,
time gap,
longing.
Sabre wind around
dull teeth and
relations of firth
Red Fire Almighty,
save my teeth, and agree.
I, Red, Four, Eight, One,
armor is real entity,
are is night,
commodity,
I love you,
Wyoming.

My Forfeiture

At port beach with tinsure
I can't see but what to the fog?
I come back with all these,
I saw more anger after his, there,
forfeiture.
I would not forfeit known race,
I would not forfeit known visions
of mine, but so, there lost on me.
I was upset, so I take more meth,
this does as vows,
this does as vows.
Take this as my gift to you,
my forfeiture.

Courage, Recovery, Time

See a memory,

my foggy lamp outside

my parent's house for the winter.

I lackluster spent smoking pot

spent minerals, open eyes

open inside afterwards,

I spent time, body's spent cash.

Afterwards all that

is left, is you.

Drinking in tandem with thirst

and fore-longing,

I spit into a vial,

my cigarette makes me sick.

This fall, I will fly an airplane,

through the cloudy tunnel

over the ocean to London,

where I left a letter

to you, and my absent thoughts.

I will remember eight

illuminated sides, nine parts

including time, I cry in the

musician's apartment

about premonitions and my

helpless soul, high and drunk like

a ladder, speckled with paint.

Black-shiny submarine, I am a

vessel of ideologies and rasp,

my throat is a plant like weed,

sticky and green, an ocean barge.
I left this space with a calm letter
weighed down in the wind from my window
with my right-hand palm.
When I come by I will read you
what I wrote, and it will resemble
the present actions of loss,
desolated and full of mirth, belonging to you,
and life, this too is desolate but
only through me, it belongs to you.
I admire a spent cigarette butt in the
ashtray as courage completes
it's song and belonging to me,
I like to admire this scene
like wave's move along a beach,
I will visit the bottom of the ocean.
America, I left the letter like
I write to homage and the future,
I write to myself, and picture
a sensical series of events that still
belong to me, even as love sets
behind the horizon, a ship at harbor
I find playing it's one solitary tuneful
song in the water,
I find I don't care for any gift
of romance, too deep in the water,
solitary photographs of weak straw,
my rodale in crimson lamp-light
at night, I am only like yours,
belonging to both God and misery
and fate, only three of radio-courage

turning into dawn tomorrow,
new photographs of straw,
a picture of my country and
it's letter monolithic,
you are looking at merely
a photograph of straw, myself
like the Methuselah, a pyre of
scepters, and walks to the store, or around town.
Quiet courage keeps me still.
Left after this, is you.
My army is a medical sense,
and an ignorance of speed.
My letter regards this as coincidence,
and a raw destiny like fireworks.
Love is real, it is dawn, the new day
of beauty and stillness of heart, the
solidified feeling of my heart.
Loss is unreal, unrelenting.
Fly the airplane, and to five directions
time will persevere.
Love will be recovery,
also like dawn, where you
fly over Wyoming,
missing pieces of straw.

Time Glass

I spoke into a glass,
it beheld of me to drink.
I beget four loose forms,
air and water, distant love,
why so long until I dream?

My Remembering Rodale Necklace Pendant

I look for moonlight to

activate my amethyst and aquamarine

crystals in my necklace pendant,

and find my walk too late in the

night for the moon to be out,

the moon that was following me

earlier, one or two mornings ago.

The moon must have fallen over the edge

of the Earth,

flat Earth,

a garden of those who do not wish to

destroy us, the keepers of the garden.

Without the garden's keepers,

the Earth would be either like before or

more likely newly a dry, gray plane,

rocky yet with no Forsythia or other

plants, solidified with maybe a new song,

from the Earth? or from the lions?

From the flies or the spiders, or both?

I walk towards town,

looking for amethyst, or aquamarine,

again.

Missouri, Trance Number One

Count thee thy number of ways
I love you. I may give back more energy
than I consume, walking back
from town I guess this.
Just being clean, and organized,
and nice, surely is energy that is useful.
I am a black shiny submarine,
further, desolate, longing.
I am a ship at harbor,
Tomatoes, Onions, calm quiet and forgiving.
I wash my teeth and think of a
vision for tomorrow, and smoke
to relieve my flesh.
One, two, three, four, five…
Forgiving.

Looking for Love, A Moonswept Hot Ash

I have seen

multiple pillars, of Religion,

about me, tome, and forever at once.

The inner Id and self,

receiving Gold water from

everlasting God with his five ships,

forever at once, a sound,

of a solitary drum,

and my breath as I awake.

What is a river to God?

Is it five sticks, that I skate on?

or is it flowing from my tongue?

I cast a spell on my bracelet,

it holds three forms,

heaven, of the spirit,

power, of the eye, Palandir,

and myself, of the flesh, and under-wraps.

Gold river is remarkable

light-shift and green whelks at the sea;

forlonging, ever-tide, me.

Two Floods of Emotions, By a Golden Bowl

As of ever my Forsythius, crow's call,

my mental health a matter of conquest,

I debate I am not sick, though

my psychiatrist insists I am mentally ill.

Depression calls me forlorn and beaten,

I told myself that "what if…I find nobody…

or no-one wants me, life is short, I could die, alone."

Alone is the Hades flag of conquestian symmetry, or conquest,

I see thee, I speak of thee, I smoketh thee,

and I return to my home, that (north) way!

I persist that twin sabres crossed

I remember, over a red cross, does enough,

then two scepters and a golden ring,

Forsith, it is gold that remembers it's form and attitude

over land, I remember that I

am not depressed. I spoke of compassion

and lived towards a golden Sun.

I remark Heraclitus serves ye, a mark of the Sun,

Towards center to the right, do I look right ever?

I look left and right as I walk places,

opposite my bed in my bedroom is a dresser drawers,

I need some flowers,

this fall season real

to look at nothing under the Sun.

Amazed Thought, Kingdom Sequoia

In Kingdom Sequoia

I met a girl from California

who changed my life.

I play with making words with silence,

your hair and bonds make me

pattern like rain amongst the day and night,

with the electric lamps in a line down the road.

Kingdom Sequoia, be my next rodale lusty, dawn sun,

Kingdom Saffron, in the quaint shape of space.

If I was to want you so badly,

disappearing els of time,

Kingdom of goddesses of time,

chance, dusty changing night,

chance, a river of Kingdoms run.

Kingdom Sequoia II

Lender and the world

Sabre and the world

I lend you the world

I find a sabre in the ground.

Beautiful sender and the world, I lay my sabre down.

Helios Lenders

Lender and the world

Sabre and the world

I find a sabre in the ground

and tooth it, some totalities absolute,

lewd and bard, it needs more axiom at the hilt, (tape

at the handle), lily and dandy lion and time cometh,

as usual, I spoke and lent a shape

of dark night, on some night we were all really reaching new heights,

naked soil is only ash at its lender,

like aviourous, aiortaed, aimaed,

oil on the ground like pavement, lit by rows of electric lamps,

excited, I lain my sabre down

and crossed my heart with love,

again as I walk out each morning.

Hollow Looking Glass, Coming Home After Arriving In My Room

For (little sailing mast, land leading sound), young goddess,
(mizzen-mast straight) a looking glass.
I give you these perfumes and things,
to tell you some words of thy love for you.
(modes of silver dark sign for us to say) metal-opium,
pitchers thee is (quietly you branching), tea I spill around my
coffee mug, to spill over my rim onto my bed-stand,
(First alternate visual moment I have to stay for), myself (First of our sep-
tural movement), gold and
green, (First costume of a burning vision of mine), love enumered by
light and tears mine forever if peace (idea of here to us) life (is ideas of the
vision of this) thirst I had that day for wanting you,
and all the love I have to give you, my only desire as of
counting real things,
goddess of time.

Three Towers, Snow Bottle Forest and Five Sailing Ships, Inside Me

I love you like the rain clears

from a small patch of gold in the sun,

you are my destiny, you are my star,

you are my wonder, you are my world.

Call, so said call thine hourus,

said shiny hourous thee calls on heares't

throat to flame; I flame misery: call me, again.

Nary a divisive thought, of one I only

think I want you to consider thinking of me

the same way I lust for your heart,

find me unprepared and turn my head towards

your face, and tell me how you feel.

A peaceful dove of foggy early morning's memory

will breath my lips are to taste this

forest's snow ships shape sails, a neuron,

inside me. Smoking like embers, five rodales

each a sliver of light from a lens,

paths around my home like notes from a sailor

to the land, rodale of love, sound full of stars,

my night sky full of brilliant stars!

I ask for each of my ribs to breath sail wind

to the top of my eye, crossing into the realm

of two people, ever crossing home.

Poem

I love you like the rain o'er the ocean,

more than beans and rice.

Because beans and rice is boring and the rain

and my tears trickle like stars,

I hope you love me too,

like lust, its one, my saffron lusty one,

more badly, of lust's resting els, loves more.

Poem II

When I look to my right,
it is always you leaving,
when I look to my left,
it is just my stuff, soundless and curt.
In the early morning,
there is the picture of no lover
red and grays like little poems,
windy, soundless, and curt.

More, Ignorant Self-America

Sometimes even when I'm alone,
the noise of my mind filling in what I think are
other's judgements of me grown to a painful loud crashing sounds,
for some reason I believe I am hated by everybody.
Maybe I am cursed, or just mostly unlucky.
I could just be mentally-tripping on my latent acid and,
think this way through seeing angry hallucinations, angry at me.
I once did partake in the dissemination of that idea,
I did try to ask others why I felt this way, like the world
was against me, but I don't anymore.
Not that I don't still wonder why or if, just that
so many answers were the same, if anybody listened
at all.
Sweet chrysanthemum, and of the holy ambigram sight and lattices of as-
trology and psychic selves, sully.
I do teach, realms of obvious and burning words, for all they're sully.
I see one sully's myself in crude contexts
this means I was just discussed earlier in a mood or tone of some
disliking, creative comfort is two shields,
one on my right arm, to see with, raised above my head
so I can see, or even move, (and so I am able to speak),
one in my left hand overing myself low to
prevent my subject in conversation to strike me accidentally,
when they least may expect to
find me a foe.
And emotions of the heaviest mail I have worn.
I carry no swords or knives,
maces, axes, or bows,
guns, grenades, or bombs,
missiles, planes, or boats
or even the written page;
God has write struggled (and been)
above me, I am
like an inert orange fruit,
sweet inside me, love is dark, sightless,
above me.

The Remarkable War, Quietest, Sound Explaining Sky

Quietest, the colossal looking army on the
television raised their guns and shouted.
Loudest, my homeland's colossal terror by men
films bombs exploding on the same television,
and my leaders explaining why.
"Quoweep," "quoweep," "quoweep," a summer morning's bird's call.
"Thump," "thump," "thump," "swishah-d," "click," "swish-d," myself re-
turning to bed,
retiring for the night.
Quietest, is myself at light.

Poetry Lesson Number One, If You Don't Try, At the Very Least it May Be Poetic

Any poem can be written from your words,

as long as you say what you meant,

as magnets and planets and you, will write all the rest.

Turning north, I save spake on the desert, of Jade Marks,

my words as shields, my mind of swords,

as if I was the only one present.

Three oceans, Four Friends, Eight books,

at night is the common place I wept.

My mind full of swords.

My house full of doers, and boards.

Four minds, five finders, three planes,

English, my triangle quotes to spread sonic and meanings and flowery

branches of mastery

music of my love of thee,

but not in the desert.

Like in my Rohrshach in a dream,

"The Secrets of the World."

The Joker of lost companions, or worse, sluethic loves.

The Joker always looks at me after correcting me

and waits for me to accept to be bargaining with submissionary language,

from my newly shaken eyes and timid mouth,

the Joker, one eye is always following you.

The desert does not make this better.

The Joker, weak or invisible in the desert, he is

invisible or worse on the shore.

The Joker carries three emblems,

ensuring the mind never completes a couplet of notes

sounds and relieves the muscles of
loners, the book-read, couples, and armies;
that his work here is done,
if you spot him at all.
The Joker is a book of details, and a trifecta of colors
or moods, beware; none of his words are legible and his
mood is really just to entertain you.
There is no meaning to the Joker.
If there is any character you want to avoid playing as, it is the Joker.
Derelict Sun, tin can moon-star lamps,
the desert.
Diptych of stars,
17 breaths.
If absolute stars,
fallen soldier, civilian, painted stars rodale of words,
it is the Joker,
and crying is the only sound so real if telling myself quieter sully phrases
than this, hold on to your problems and come away with me!
I write any poem
if death may take me alone, may my heart grow fonder,
and English poetry say
sweet rose, what blooms in fire from pink palms and fingers in the summer
Sun:
people of love.

Gold Plated With Diamonds

Day 2: I need to remark on my roommate

as a friend, at least as of yet and for now,

despite how her female beauty brings me great joy,

and how with us two, together, I feel like I actually own

something (my house), instead of hiding or wasting my time

somewhere…

But, I am more disturbed and desperate than you ever thought.

No, I am more disturbed and desperate than I ever would be.

I think I need to get out of your way.

I should get out of your way.

Here in my lonely starboard bow bedroom, nobody can return here

to me,

Nobody knows that I am here.

Elements of gold know no other lover,

Sanguine-gold suitor, disparate parade of none-other,

could I ever remit to my evening ship's divulger?

A golden porthole into sweet west's last remnant tickles

of love.

Shiny black machine, due wept

with all my black detail-saving photographs of nobody.